Why White Guys Play Golf!

Why White Guys Play Golf!

James Lull

Illustrations by James Lull, Jessica Helms and Lawrence Seeberger, Jr.

East Side Books
San Jose, California USA

Copyright © 1999 by James Lull. All rights reserved.

No part of this publication may be reproduced, stored in a retrieval system or transmitted in any form or by any means, electronic, mechanical, photocopying, recording or otherwise, without the prior permission of the publisher.

Published in the United States by:

East Side Books
PO Box 3417
San Jose, CA 95156-3417
USA

www.whiteguygolf.com

For information on bulk purchase for education, business or promotional purposes, contact the publisher at the above address or web site.

Library of Congress Catalog Card Number 98-96456

Lull, James.
   Why White Guys Play Golf!/by James Lull
   1. Golf 2. Humor 3. Popular Culture

ISBN 0-9666552-0-6

Production Coordinator: Barbara Day Zinicola
Printed in the United States of America

You're
on the tee,
fellas.
Have a
good one...

So,
why *do* white guys play golf?

Because white guys believe in family values...

Because white guys seek inner peace and tranquility...

Because white guys like to show off their really cool outfits...

Because white guys protect what they love...

Because white guys stay focused on their work...

Because white guys understand the enormous potential of the human mind...

Because white guys enjoy a walk in the woods...

Because white guys never drink and drive...

Because white guys give orders with authority...

Because white guys believe in fair play...

Because white guys have realistic expectations...

Because white guys know golf is just a game...

Because white guys work constantly to improve their situations...

Because white guys respect the law...

Because white guys never go anywhere without a good map...

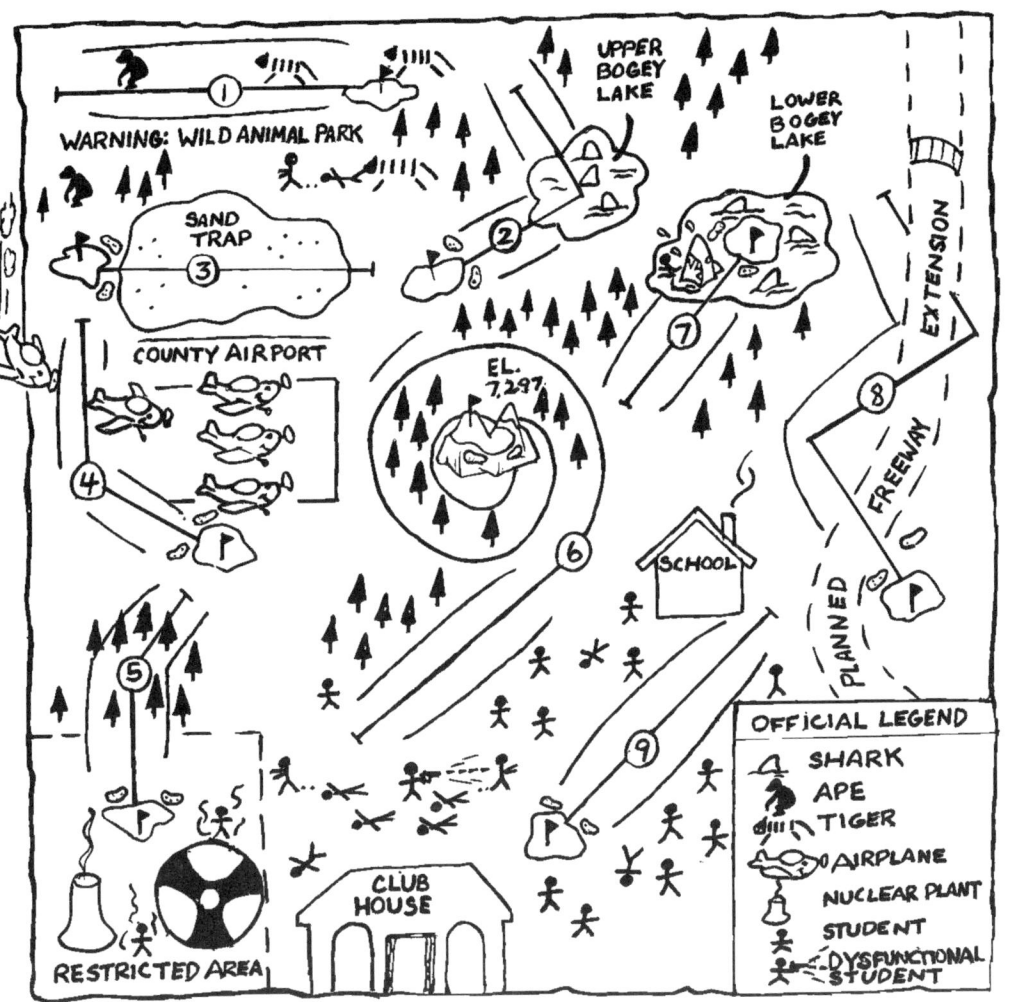

Because white guys like to get in one last practice swing...

Because white guys analyze things extremely well...

Because white guys are prompt and well-prepared...

Because white guys support institutions of higher learning...

Because white guys lay it all on the line...

Because white guys exercise regularly...

Because white guys know the worst day at golf is better than the best day at work...

Because white guys honor superior performances...

Because white guys finish what they begin...

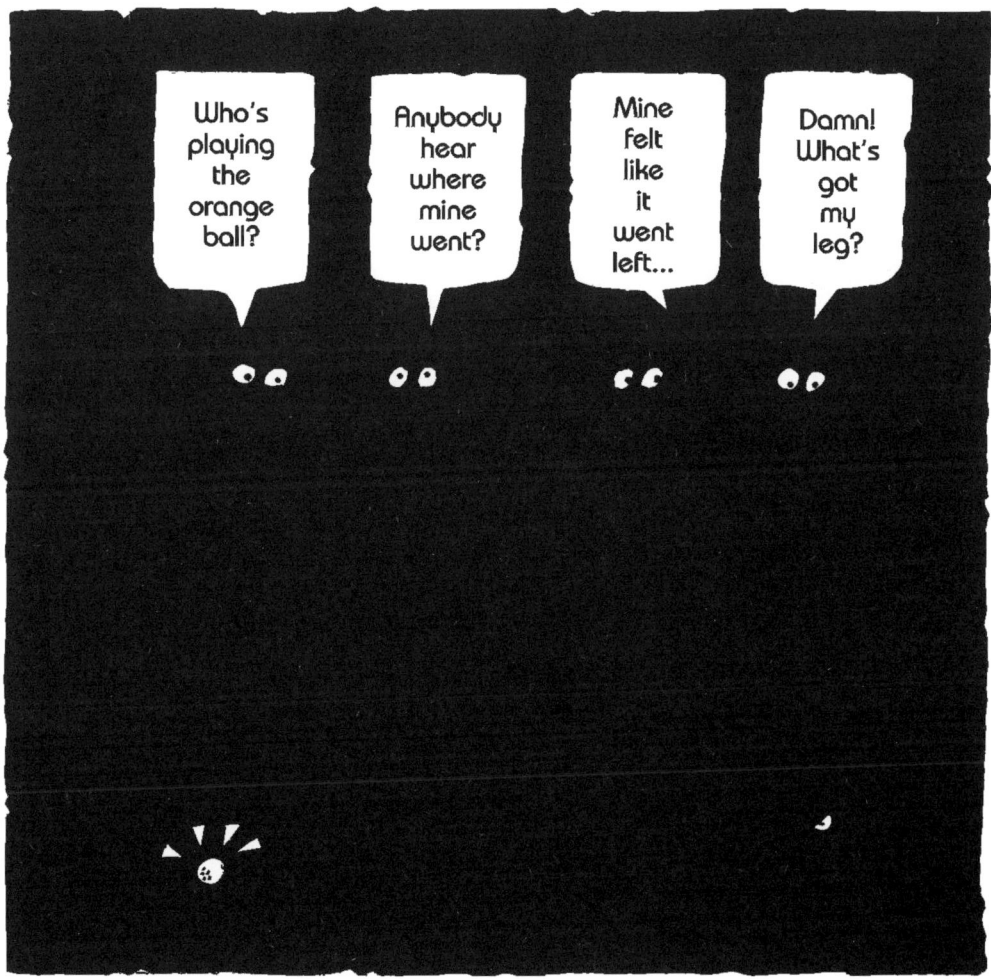

Because white guys know when to punish themselves...

Because white guys want to help him track down the real killers...

Because white guys enjoy water sports...

Because white guys enjoy adding to their impressive toy collections...

Because white guys insist on quality time...

Because white guys look forward to family vacations...

Because white guys are true believers...

Because white guys gladly give free advice...

Because white guys keep their priorities in order...

Because white guys can always find the beach...

Because white guys support each other in a crisis...

Because white guys know success is close at hand...

Because white guys worship the great outdoors...

Because white guys don't waste those precious moments at home...

Because white guys know
where the real deals are made...

Because white guys believe in a healthy, well-balanced diet...

Because white guys hate to lose old friends...

Because white guys are not easily discouraged...

Because white guys step right up to the challenge...

Because white guys keep an eye on global trends...

Because white guys know that timing is everything...

Because white guys are in touch with their feminine side...

Because white guys like to really get to know each other...

Because white guys know what it means to scramble...

Because white guys are good with garden tools...

Because white guys always have an alternative plan...

Because white guys play sports with finesse and intelligence ...

Because white guys know it's never too late for a second chance...

Because white guys appreciate the delicate balance of Earth's natural resources...

Because white guys enjoy the privileges of country club living...

Because white guys are natural athletes...

Because white guys know that progress can be slow...

Because white guys know who their friends are...

Because white guys can always get a foursome together...

Because white guys respect each other's space...

Because white guys stay cool under pressure...

Because white guys know how to get away from it all...

Because white guys keep their thoughts to themselves...

Because white guys like an audience they can impress...

Because white guys give themselves to nature...

Because white guys celebrate their roots...

Because white guys don't have many sports left...

Because white guys know the true meaning of the holidays...